MI VIDA LOCA

Eric Overmyer

BROADWAY PLAY PUBLISHING INC
New York
www.broadwayplaypublishing.com
info@broadwayplaypublishing.com

MI VIDA LOCA
© Copyright 1991 by Eric Overmyer

First printing: July 2013
I S B N: 978-0-88145-581-6

Book design: Marie Donovan
Page make-up: Adobe Indesign
Typeface: Palatino
Printed and bound in the U S A

BY ERIC OVERMYER
PUBLISHED BY
BROADWAY PLAY PUBLISHING INC

NATIVE SPEECH (1984)
ON THE VERGE (1986)
IN PERPETUITY THROUGHOUT
THE UNIVERSE (1989)
IN A PIG'S VALISE (1989)
DARK RAPTURE (1993)
DON QUIXOTE DE LA JOLLA (1993)
THE HELIOTROPE BOUQUET BY SCOTT JOPLIN
AND LOUIS CHAUVIN (1993)
FIGARO/FIGARO (1996)
ALKI (1996)
AMPHITRYON (1996)

An earlier version of MI VIDA LOCA was commissioned by South Coast Rep.

MI VIDA LOCA was first produced by the Manhattan Theatre Club (Lynne Meadow, Artistic Director; Barry Grove, Managing Director). The first performance, at City Center Stage II, was on 8 May 1990. The cast and creative contributors were as follows:

AJAY	Robert Lansing
LULU	Caris Corfman
PACO	John Slattery
DIANA	J Smith-Cameron
MAGGIE	Barbara Barrie
BUBBA	Lou Milione
Director	David Warren
Scenery	James Noone
Costumes	David Woolard
Lighting	Donald Holder
Original music & sound	Mark Bennett
Production stage manager	Richard Hester

This play is for Caris Corfman and Kent Paul.

ACT ONE

Scene 1

(A long sagging porch. Lots of stuff. Rusting junk. Bikes, volleyball poles, cardtables, rakes, basketball hoops.)

(A hammock)

(An expanse of brilliant white sand. Behind and beyond, dense dark-green, wet woods.)

(Dawn. Sunny. Distantly, the ocean. Seabirds. Early spring.)

*(A*JAY, *late fifties, comes out on the porch in pajamas, robe, smoking a pipe. He surveys the territory distractedly for a moment, then descends the stairs to the sand. He scrawls his name in the sand with one slipper, admires his graffiti, and wanders off toward the ocean.)*

*(L*ULU *comes out onto the porch. Early thirties, dark blonde hair bleached blonder, too much eye makeup.)*

LULU: I'm standing in the driveway, watching the dog eat grass. Thinking about nothing in particular. Thinking about this guy I met last night at The Flame. Thinking about is he gonna call me, or should I call him. Or should I just forget it. Thinking. And I hear this noise. It's way far away. Nnnnn. High-pitched. Nnnnnnn. Kind of a mosquito-like noise. Nnnnnnn. A hum. A drone. Nnnnnnn. Like a dentist's drill. And it's getting closer and closer, and louder and louder. And I look down at the beach towards Alki—and the sunbathers are looking around, and back up over the hill, and I turn to look, too. It's a plane. A sea plane. Pontoons. Y'know? And the nnnnn is all kind of wobbly and spluttery now, and the plane's got a bad case of the shakes or something. And then it starts going nnnn...spppttt...nnnn...spptttt...and it's going for the Sound, but it's not gonna make it no way. And it's headed right at me. And I'm paralyzed, trying to remember what you're supposed to do in situations like these. But I can't. Nnnn...sppppttt. Getting real loud. And I'm standing there thinking what if that guy I met last night at the Flame calls me. What am I gonna do? And the plane stops nnnnnning and sppttting and goes completely silent. Engine just dies. And it sails over the top of my house. Whoosh. Clips the T V antenna. And then it kinda coasts real quiet and smooth into the neighbors' garage. Whoosh. Kaboom. Whoosh again. Different whoosh. Big ball of orange fire 'n black smoke. Goes up like a roman candle. Totals the place. Wow.

(Pause)

LULU: That kind of stuff is always happening to me.

(Pause. Notices AJAY's *name on the sand.)*

LULU: Ajay. What a card. Anyway. Mi vida loca. My crazy life. My crazy fucking life. Whooosh. *(She walks off toward the ocean.)*

*(*PACO *enters, carrying an overnight bag. He stops and looks at the house. Walks up onto the porch, drops his pack.)*

PACO: That smell. I'd recognize that smell on Zanzibar. Degenerating gene pool. Brr. *(Peers into the house. Decides not to go in. Turns and walks to the front porch. Looks at the sand. Sees* AJAY's *name.)*

PACO: Ajay. What a card.

(DIANA *comes out of the house.* PACO's *presence surprises her.*)

DIANA: Oh.

PACO: Hi.

DIANA: Good morning. I was just looking for Ajay. He's got to get ready.

PACO: He was here.

DIANA: Where'd he go?

PACO: Dunno. He left his mark.

DIANA: I see.

PACO: I'm Paco.

DIANA: You don't look like a Paco.

PACO: Do I know you?

DIANA: I'm Diana.

PACO: Ajay's companion.

DIANA: Caretaker. Companion sounds—

PACO: Yes, it does. We'll have to come up with another term. Guardian angel.

DIANA: Some guardian. My charge has wandered off who knows where.

PACO: Check the attic? He used to hide in the attic. Used to pretend to live up there. The monster in the attic.

DIANA: Boarded up.

PACO: It's not what you look like, it's what you feel like. I feel like a Paco.

DIANA: Fair enough.

PACO: Seen Lulu?

DIANA: Not today.

PACO: Out all night?

(DIANA *shrugs.*)

PACO: What a question. Lulu. How is Lulu? Got a job?

DIANA: No.

PACO: Par. You get along with old Lu?

DIANA: She and your father are very close.

PACO: Two peas in a pod, Maggie says.

DIANA: Well. She resents my presence, I think.

PACO: She thinks she can look after Ajay.

DIANA: She thinks I'm unnecessary. A waste of money.

PACO: But when she's here, she's out all night. Every night.

DIANA: Far as I can tell.

PACO: Lulu's got stamina. Girl can't help it. Born to rock and roll. Unnecessary. Unnecessary. So one winter in New York, lots of snow, lots of ice, and I go out for a cafe con leche and a macaroon, which I could still eat in those days without causing too much damage to my triglycerides level, and a paper. You got time for a story?

DIANA: Don't see why not.

PACO: So I walk up the street, heading for my favorite Dominican bakery, which isn't there anymore, and I see this guy in a car, this black guy, and he's rocking this B M W back and forth, and he's obviously a lunatic and not the owner of record, if you know what I mean.

DIANA: How do you know?

PACO: How do I know? How do I know? This is pre-gentrification West End Avenue in the Hundreds, the neighborhood is crawling with hallucinating paranoid schizophrenics who've been released as quote unquote

not dangerous by state institutions that've run out of
money, and so given the number of deranged maniacs
in the vicinity, plus my man's matted dreadlocks,
drool, snot, assorted barks, chirps, and growls, plus
the way he's trying to shift gears without using the
clutch, causing a ferocious crunchy grinding sound,
leads me to believe this is not his own personal B M W,
and he himself is just a tiny bit disturbed. At least this
morning.

DIANA: Everybody has bad days.

PACO: Plus he doesn't have an ignition key. And he
can't understand why the car won't go.

DIANA: Right.

PACO: Plus the window's shattered, and there's glass
all over the street.

DIANA: Okay. Okay.

PACO: It's the little things. The tiny clues the observant
witness ferrets out.

DIANA: Gotcha now.

PACO: Just an educated guess. Circumstantial, but—

DIANA: I'll buy it.

PACO: So. I'm trying to decide what to do. The car is
rocking, I'm about to go call the cops, and these two
guys, obviously father and son, in matching camel hair
coats and black homburgs, come out of the building.
Very stylish. Accountants, lawyers, architects. And
they look at this wild man of Borneo in their B M W.
Hey, do you see what I see sort of thing. Very low
key. Gee, Dad, there seems to be a lunatic in the car,
Dad. Yes, Seymour, gosh darn it, I wish he'd use the
clutch, I've told your mother about the very same
thing. So they start banging on the door and yelling at
this guy, who's oblivious, just ignores 'em, and keeps

gnashing them gears. And then Junior goes back into
the building and calls the cops, and comes back, and
they're wondering what to do, and all of a sudden he
loses interest. The Wild Man. Stops shifting the gears,
gets out of the car, and wanders up the street. So, what
do father and son do?

DIANA: I give up. What?

PACO: The cops are on their way, right? And they
called 'em. And this lunatic, who's big, by the way, six
something, is wandering off into the sunset. So what
do Mr. and Mr. Solid Upstanding Citizen do? They get
in their car and drive off.

DIANA: New York. Unbelievable.

PACO: Hey, it's Saturday, they've got places to go,
people to see. So they drive off, broken window and
all, and I think, holy shit. Maybe this guy's had his
episode for the day, and maybe not. So I follow him up
the street. And he's ambling along, singing to himself,
moaning, who can tell, weaving back and forth across
the pavement, slipping and sliding, and all of a sudden
he bursts! I mean, bursts! Pops! Like somebody zapped
his poor sore fucked-up brain tissue with a jolt of pure
voltage. And he takes off around the corner cursing
and shouting, towards Riverside Park. And I hear this
terrible commotion, and I run after him, and as I get
to the corner I practically bump into Mister Wild Man
of Borneo coming back the other way, and he flies
past me, and then this white guy, grad student type,
face all bloody comes busting by after him, and it's
like a cartoon, their wheels are spinning, and the Grad
Student says to me as he goes by, "Groceries! Get my
groceries!" which shows some presence of mind, if you
ask me. And I go around the corner and pick up his
groceries, which are scattered all over the sidewalk.
Broken eggs and blood on the snow. Bright red. Bright

yellow. Off white. Still life. New York Mugging. It was perfect. So I pick up this carton of milk, it's leaking a little, and this loaf of bread and I hurry back to West End to see what's going down, and up at the next corner there are a couple of cop cars, and they've got the guy. He's got his hands up on the car and his legs spread and they're frisking him. So I walk up and give the Grad Student his milk, and he says, "Thanks, man," and he's got a pretty bad bloody nose, it looks broken, and he says "The guy just attacked me," and the cops are standing around debating whether to take the Wild Man to jail or to the hospital, and one cop is saying, "Deranged. The guy's deranged," and they ask me to come to the station to be a witness. And then a little burst of electricity must go through The Wild Man again, he has a idea, you can almost see the lightbulb come on, and he reaches for the cop's gun. Just grabs for it. Wham wham wham wham wham. The cop hits the guy with his night stick five or six times, so fast it's a blur. I've never seen anything like it. Pure reflex. And they all jump him, throw him face down in the snow, and handcuff his hands behind his back. And there's blood everywhere. All over the snow.

DIANA: Jesus.

PACO: Yeah. And after they finished beating the poor sucker's head to a bloody pulp, and he's lying there bleeding in the snow, he's moaning "Un-necessary. Un-necessary. Un-necessary." Over and over. Really singing it. A mantra. "Un-necessary. Un-necessary. Un-necessary." So, anyway, I go to the precinct house, where I learn a new word, perp, tell my story to some desk jockey who couldn't care less, and go home three hours later. Never heard another word about it. Don't know what became of the Wild Man, the Grad Student. Don't know if the case ever went to trial. Anyway, just goes to show, you never know what's gonna happen to you when you go out for a cup of coffee in New York.

DIANA: You ever get that cafe con leche?

PACO: No. No, never did, come to think of it. Never did. I did however find out the answer to a question I'd been wondering about for a long long time. What would happen if you reached out and touched a cop's gun.

DIANA: Seems pretty obvious.

PACO: You never had that impulse?

DIANA: No.

PACO: Cop walking in front of you down the street. At the next table. Strap hanging in the subway. Reach out and touch that gun?

DIANA: No.

PACO: Well, good. Don't.

DIANA: Did I miss the point?

PACO: I don't think so. Of what?

DIANA: Why did you tell me that story?

PACO: Oh. Unnecessary. Lulu. That word. That's all.

DIANA: What do you think? Am I necessary?

PACO: I assume so.

DIANA: Then I better go find him.

PACO: He'll be back. Ajay's slow and steady.

DIANA: He is so slow. He's late for everything.

PACO: The family joke about Ajay. He'd be late for his own funeral. And he was. I mean. *(Pause)* I mean. Not to his. To Jimmy's. You've heard about Jimmy?

DIANA: Maggie talks about him. Lulu too.

PACO: Yes. Well.

(Pause)

DIANA: So you were late?

PACO: Oh, yes. They were all waiting for us. A church full of people. We even got lost on the way. We'd never been there before. But we were beyond embarrassment. If there were a family coat of arms, that would be the motto. In Latin. Beyond embarrassment. I could use a good cafe con leche right now.

DIANA: You're pretty wired already.

PACO: Visiting the old homestead's a natural rush.

DIANA: Understand. Listen, I've really got to go find Ajay.

PACO: He's probably just down to the beach.

(AJAY enters, unnoticed by DIANA and PACO.)

PACO: It's his ritual trek. He'll be back. Poor Ajay. You know, he bought this place as beachfront property. Sight unseen. When he got out here he found out he was on a dune back in the woods and the ocean was a good half mile away. Story of his life.

AJAY: Story of my life. Hello, Paul, when did you get in?

PACO: Hi, Pop. Ajay.

(AJAY and PACO shake hands.)

PACO: Just now.

AJAY: That your Buick out front?

PACO: Yeah.

AJAY: Always bought Fords. Always voted Republican and always bought Fords.

PACO: I wouldn't brag about it. Besides, you told me you voted for Truman.

AJAY: I did. Yes, that's true. I did. I was just back from the war, and a little plain speaking seemed like a good idea. What a joke. I didn't think Dewey was telling the truth. Met Diana?

DIANA: He has.

AJAY: She's been a big help. And I didn't buy this property sight unseen. I saw it.

PACO: You saw it? You saw it? How could anyone? You saw it? You always told me you bought it sight unseen. This fabulous windswept beachfront property.

AJAY: I saw it. I liked it. I bought it.

PACO: You knew how far it was to the beach.

AJAY: Sure. Even I can find the Pacific Ocean.

PACO: And all that guff about the Great Swindle?

AJAY: Just guff. I got tired of all the commentary about how far it was to the beach, so I made up that song and dance about a swindle. People enjoy that kind of line. Makes 'em feel superior. `Course, it is beachfront, technically. There is not one single solitary house between us and the water. Besides, I always figured sooner or later we'd be on the ocean, what with erosion and all. Now it's just a question of who's eroding faster, me or the beach.

PACO: No contest.

AJAY: I am making my comeback here today, Paul.

PACO: That's what I hear. Congratulations.

AJAY: Thanks. It was either that or kill myself.

DIANA: Excuse me. Ajay, I'll get your stuff together.

(She exits inside.)

PACO: Is that true? Or are you just being funny? Some of that famous dry wit.

AJAY: Some of that. Some of the other.

(*Pause*)

PACO: Well. Jesus. So. Wanna tell me about it?

AJAY: What's to tell? Chronically depressed. That's what Doctor T. tells me.

PACO: I could have told you that. What about your lawyers?

AJAY: They seem to think it would be a good idea, too.

(*Pause*)

PACO: Come on, Ajay. Jesus. Getting anything out of you is like pulling teeth. Details. How long, what's supposed to happen, that sort of thing.

AJAY: It's four weeks. They put you on a program. They wean you.

PACO: What's it called?

AJAY: The Pain Clinic.

PACO: The Pain Clinic. Sounds inviting.

AJAY: They inflict it in order to eliminate it.

PACO: That's good, Ajay. I'm glad to see your aphoristic faculties are unimpaired.

AJAY: Oh, they're impaired, Paul. They are definitely impaired. I am in a deep fog here most of the time. I am in my own private rain forest. Fog, mist, moss, and air. The dead center of the Olympic mountains.

(*Pause*)

PACO: You used to tell me you won a medal in the 1944 Olympics. Remember?

AJAY: Bronze in wrestling.

PACO: Usually. Sometimes a silver in swimming.

AJAY: I was a good swimmer.

PACO: Sure.

AJAY: Dynamite swimmer. Fair wrestler.

PACO: So this place is at the University. The Pain Clinic.

AJAY: Right. Doctor. T. He says it's my last chance.

PACO: Don't say that.

AJAY: I don't. He does.

(Pause)

PACO: Ajay, I wish— *(Beat)* What's the program?

AJAY: Methadone and counseling. Dope and psychobabble. A couple of times a day they give you this thing they call a Pain Cocktail.

(Pause)

(PACO waits.)

AJAY: Mostly dope at first, and a little bit of methadone and gradually they reverse the proportions, and eventually phase out the morphine. I understand the methadone makes you feel like you have a bad case of the flu. For the rest of your life.

PACO: The rest of your life?

AJAY: Maybe. Once you're on methadone you have to kick that. Some do, some don't.

PACO: Hey, life's a bitch, and then you die.

AJAY: But first you have root canal.

(AJAY and PACO both laugh.)

PACO: Look. Lulu's gonna drive you up to Seattle?

AJAY: Yeah.

PACO: Why don't you let me drive you?

AJAY: No, that's alright. Your sister insists. *(Beat)* Paul, what are you doing here?

PACO: Came to see you off.

(Pause)

AJAY: Alright. Well, I should get ready. Get my things together. Get dressed. I'm running a little late.

PACO: Ajay. What are you up to?

AJAY: What do you mean?

PACO: I mean, how much are you doing?

AJAY: Oh, an unconscionable amount. 65 grains a pop. A many-times-lethal dose, according to Doctor T. I've got a helluva habit.

PACO: Jesus. It never levels off, does it?

AJAY: No, it doesn't seem to. You'd think, after all these years.

PACO: I thought. Well. After you build up a tolerance.

AJAY: It doesn't slacken.

PACO: No.

AJAY: It doesn't level off. It just grows and grows. It yawns. If there's one thing I've got, it's a habit that just won't quit. *(Beat)* I thought. I do have a few more years left. Let's see if I can come up for a little air.

PACO: Good luck.

AJAY: Yes, sir. *(He starts to go in the house.)*

PACO: Ajay. Diana's taking care of things. Stay here and talk to me.

AJAY: I have to get dressed.

PACO: Go in your jammies. They're just gonna put you back in them. *(Pause)* Why not start now? Get a jump on the program.

AJAY: Paul. You don't understand.

PACO: No.

AJAY: It's a long drive. I want to be comfortable.

PACO: Sure.

(*At the door,* AJAY *turns.*)

AJAY: Get it while you can. (*He exits.*)

PACO: Shit. (*He walks up onto the porch and flops in the hammock.*) Shit. Shit. Shit.

(LULU *enters.*)

LULU: You're in a good mood.

PACO: Hey, Lulu. What's shaking?

LULU: Paco. When'd you get in.

PACO: Last night.

LULU: Bullshit.

PACO: How would you know?

LULU: I know when you're full of shit. Which is all the time.

PACO: Very discriminating, very discerning, very perspicacious.

LULU: Bullshit. Where's Pop?

PACO: Inside. Getting loaded.

LULU: Give him a break. It's his last day of relative well-being. From here on in, he's gonna feel like cream of shit.

PACO: How do you know?

LULU: I drink methadone for breakfast, smartass. Doctor T told me.

PACO: You sure you're in shape to drive to Seattle?

LULU: I'm fine. I got a lot of sleep last night.

PACO: Not a wink, as the old joke goes. You seeing someone?

LULU: No. I spent last night with a total stranger. Creep. Yes, of course I'm seeing someone. Several someones.

PACO: Like 'em?

LULU: They're okay. Nothing to write home about.

PACO: Got a job?

LULU: No.

PACO: How long's it been?

LULU: I don't know.

PACO: Looking?

LULU: No.

PACO: I only ask because you owe me that money you borrowed for the rent four years ago.

LULU: One hundred and fifty dollars. B F D. I'll sell my first born.

PACO: Who'd buy it?

LULU: Very funny.

(Pause)

PACO: Bad night, huh?

LULU: I've had better.

PACO: Look. Ajay's got a habit to support. Not to mention Maggie on his back. He doesn't need you, too.

LULU: Don't lecture me, Paco.

PACO: Sorry.

LULU: Fuck you. Just fuck you. You waltz in here and start running my life. It's not fair. Go back to Sonoma. Leave me alone. It's not fair. I'm the one who had to stay here and deal with all this shit.

PACO: No you didn't. *(Silence)* Where's Maggie?

LULU: She moved out.

PACO: God, I knew it was quiet around here.

LULU: Moved down to the beach. She's convinced
Ajay's trying to kill her.

PACO: Stop.

LULU: Yeah. Maggie was talking on the phone to Aunt
Pig about the lawsuit and the divorce settlement and
so on and so forth, and Maggie got excited like she
usually does, and she pulled the phone jack out of the
wall, and the phone goes dead, and she thinks Ajay's
cut the wire, and he's gonna come in and strangle
her, and she goes screaming down the road to the
Harrisons' and tries to get them to call the police.

PACO: Jesus. She gets worse and worse.

LULU: So she moved down to the beach, and now she
only comes over when Ajay's away. Remember when
Mister Lapadura and his father-in-law broke into
the Harrisons' house in the middle of the night with
a shotgun, and threatened to rape Mrs. Harrison in
front of Mister Harrison because Mister Harrison was
having an affair with Mrs Lapadura? And you could
hear Mrs Harrison saying, "What do you think you're
doing? What do you think you're doing?" And the
cops came. And then Mrs Harrison spent the rest of the
evening screaming at Mister Harrison, "You fucked
her? How could you fuck her?" Tough way to find out
your husband's having an affair. In the middle of the
night, looking down the barrel of a twelve-gauge.

PACO: Fun never stops in the country. They're
divorced, aren't they?

LULU: They are.

PACO: So Maggie's been yakking up a storm with Aunt
Pig.

LULU: They're cooking up schemes.

PACO: What kind of schemes?

LULU: Schemes to separate Ajay from his dough.

PACO: Lovely. He doesn't even have it yet.

LULU: You'll see. In four weeks, shit's gonna hit the fan.

PACO: What happens in four weeks?

(AJAY *and* DIANA *come out of the house.* DIANA *is carrying a small suitcase.*)

LULU: When Ajay gets back.

PACO: Oh, no.

AJAY: Oh, yes, what about my getting back?

(AJAY *is "comfortable" now, far less present.*)

PACO: Ah, Lulu was just asking me to come back up in four weeks, when you get home.

AJAY: Don't bother. Unnecessary.

(DIANA *and* PACO *exchange a smile.*)

PACO: Lulu, when Ajay gets back, why don't you drive him down to see me. You'd like Sonoma, Lulu. It's got bars.

LULU: Too far. Come on, Pop.

(LULU *takes the suitcase from* DIANA.*)

PACO: Aren't you ashamed of never having been out of the great state of Washington?

LULU: I went to Ohio on the train, when I was nine, with the whole family. You may remember. You were there, even though you hate to admit it. And I visited you in Portland twice.

PACO: That's right, you did. You actually crossed the Columbia River, and nothing happened.

LULU: Come on, Pop, let's hit the road.

PACO: See you, Ajay.

AJAY: `Bye.

DIANA: Goodbye, Ajay. Good luck.

(AJAY *gives a distracted wave, walks off porch, heads off.*)

LULU: You look sharp in clothes, Pop. You should wear 'em more often. Paco, still be here when I get back?

PACO: When do you get back?

LULU: Tomorrow.

PACO: Maybe.

LULU: Don't put yourself out.

(LULU *exits after* AJAY.)

(*Long pause*)

DIANA: Walk on the beach?

PACO: Great.

(DIANA *and* PACO *stroll off the porch toward the ocean.*)

(*From the other direction* MAGGIE *enters. Fifty-five. She walks up on the porch and into the house.*)

(*Slow fade*)

Scene 2

(*Late afternoon. Shadows and sunlight. More stuff on the porch. Kitchen chairs. Pots and pans, fishing gear, boots and shoes, footballs and soccer balls.*)

(DIANA *and* PACO *are going through* AJAY's *stash.*)

PACO: You think that's it?

DIANA: I think that's it, yeah. (*She tosses several pill vials into a trash bag.*)

PACO: Hand me that screwdriver, will you?

(DIANA *hands* PACO *a screwdriver; he bends to pry open a padlock on a small refrigerator.*)

DIANA: What do you do in Sonoma?

PACO: I run a movie house. A genre movie house. Movie movies.

DIANA: B movies.

PACO: At best. Movies I want to see. Or movies I don't want to see. Ever. But I want to see their titles up on the marquee. *How to Stuff a Wild Bikini. Faster, Pussycat, Kill! Kill! Mars Needs Women.*

DIANA: I discern a theme.

PACO: Oh? Oh. Yeah. That theme. It crops up. From time to time. We show the gamut. Horror movies, film noir, sci-fi cheapies. You know. Strange cinema.

DIANA: No slasher movies, I hope.

PACO: Not in my bijoux. So American, slasher movies. Sex, a crime punishable by cinematic dismemberment.

DIANA: Glad to hear it. I was just beginning to like you. What's in there?

PACO: Suppositories.

DIANA: You're kidding.

PACO: Nope. Dilaudid suppositories.

DIANA: Dilaudid, that's not as serious, is it?

PACO: Same difference. Morphine base. Fuck. Here we go. There. *(He pops the lock open. Takes out stacks of small white boxes.)*

DIANA: Jesus. There's a shitload. So to speak.

PACO: For a rainy day.

DIANA: Prescribed by the evil doctor Clawhammer?

PACO: Clawhammer, yeah. Clammer, and not genuinely evil, I suppose, just stupid and careless and lazy. Which amounts to the same thing in a doctor, right? When you're too fucking lazy and stupid to, "a", make the right diagnosis in the first place, and "b", order the right treatment on it so it doesn't get out of hand, well—

DIANA: Evil.

PACO: Evil. But stupid.

DIANA: Twenty years of this.

PACO: That seems to be the consensus. This is what he got started on. These and the morphine sulphate tablets. Which would be my choice. (*He dumps the boxes in the trash bag.*)

DIANA: Mine, too. Uh— (*She shudders.*)

PACO: On the other hand, maybe we shouldn't knock it if we haven't tried it.

DIANA: No, thanks.

PACO: A little morphine up the—? Whaddya say?

DIANA: No. Thank you.

PACO: Okay. Our loss. Mighta been fun. Thrill of a lifetime. (*He tosses a box in the trash.*) Twenty years is a major league monkey. A lot falls by the wayside. He started missing work, coming in late. I imagine when you're in a morphine mist your work lacks, shall we say, precision. They'd send him on trips and he'd have to come home early cause he'd run out of shit. One time, he came home early from Australia. Maggie was fit to be tied. Anyway, the company finally gave him his walking papers after twelve or fourteen years of semi-loyal and less-than-reliable service. So his insurance company refuses to pay off on his retirement. Medical disability, which this clearly was. Debilitating addiction. Says take a hike, pal. So he lives on unemployment for a few years, `til that runs out, takes a job teaching at some juco in Ohio, gets fired, same deal, misses class, stoned in his trailer, comes back here, runs out of options. Like today.

DIANA: Today's different.

PACO: Yeah, well. So, anyway, the creditors are howling at the door, and he finally gets it together to sue. And the insurance company settles like that. Out of court. They knew they had no case all along. Ajay was pretty happy that day. Paid his lawyers their forty percent and came home shouting I'm retired! I'm retired! Or so I'm told. And now he's suing Clawhammer. He's litigation crazed.

DIANA: Everyone talks like it's a fait accompli.

PACO: I know. Makes me nervous. Clawhammer's own lawyers have urged him to settle. He refuses. Hasn't done anything wrong. Jerk. *(They put the rest of the drugs in the sack.)* Your turn.

DIANA: What?

PACO: You know all our secrets. Spill your guts.

DIANA: Not all, I don't think.

PACO: You will.

DIANA: Oh, boy. I can't wait. Let's see. I'm your age.

PACO: How old am I? How old do I look?

DIANA: Thirty-three.

PACO: Shit.

DIANA: I like it. I'm having a much better time now. Grew up in Sonoma County, as a matter of fact—

PACO: No kidding. Santa Rosa?

DIANA: Petaluma.

PACO: Chicken capital of the world.

DIANA: Eggs. And arm wrestling. Where's your theater?

PACO: Sebastapol.

DIANA: Oh, yeah? What's it called?

PACO: The Roxy. Roxy. Just Roxy. People say "The Roxy," but it's just—Roxy.

DIANA: Roxy hearts.

PACO: Right.

DIANA: Spent some time in Portland—

PACO: My condolences—

DIANA: Some time in New York. Worked a lot of jobs. PA for a production company, you'll like this, they made trailers for B-movies—

PACO: My favorites. I do evenings of just trailers. They're very popular.

DIANA: I imagine a lot of people would rather see the trailers than sit through the movies.

PACO: I have a loyal following. You should come down and check it out. Roxy's beautiful. Pink, blue, and coral neon. A big, old Spanish stucco Wurlitzer juke box. A dream palace of a bygone era.

DIANA: Maybe I will.

PACO: Oh, I hope so.

(Pause)

DIANA: That was fun. The P A job. Waitressing, retail, wrote speeches for a congresswoman from Queens for awhile, worked for an escort service, hooked—

PACO: Hooked? As in hooked?

DIANA: Hooked.

PACO: A hooker. I'm shocked.

DIANA: You're shocked? Coming from this family?

PACO: You're right.

DIANA: Okay then. Lots of very unlikely people have turned tricks. I used to meet them in New York.

PACO: Oh, well. New York.

DIANA: Well-known playwrights, directors. Actors and actresses—

PACO: Show business, that's not surprising.

DIANA: Stock brokers. System analysts. Diplomats. Investment bankers.

PACO: Stop. Who'd pay to fuck an investment banker? Seriously.

DIANA: You'd be surprised. I hear investment bankers are very special.

PACO: No. *(Pause)* Really? You?

DIANA: Yeah. For a few months. I just sort of fell into it.

PACO: Really.

DIANA: Yeah. Um. I don't usually tell people this. Stop looking at me.

PACO: No. Sorry. I've just never had a conversation with a hooker before.

DIANA: Paco. I'm not a hooker. I wasn't a hooker. I just hooked. For a couple of months.

PACO: What was that like?

DIANA: I don't know. It was a long time ago. I don't remember. It was okay.

PACO: Did you have a pimp?

DIANA: With a white fur coat and a purple lamé Cadillac.

PACO: You're kidding.

DIANA: It was done through the escort service. Run by a nice young lady who just graduated Bryn Mawr. It was fun. For a while. Then it stopped being fun, and I quit.

PACO: Do you hate men?

DIANA: No.

PACO: Were you abused as a child?

DIANA: No.

PACO: Do you have low self-esteem?

DIANA: No.

PACO: Did you hate the work?

DIANA: No.

PACO: Are you non-orgasmic?

DIANA: Paco.

PACO: You're not cooperating with the standard sociological profile.

DIANA: Never make assumptions.

PACO: I won't.

DIANA: I just fell into it. I'll tell you all about it. It'll make a lurid chapter in my autobiography.

PACO: Where did you live in New York?

DIANA: 98th and Broadway.

PACO: I thought you looked familiar. I used to see you on the corner of Broadway and 98th Street after midnight—

DIANA: No way.

PACO:—those skintight burgundy spandex hot pants—

DIANA: Strictly an indoor player Astroturf. Domed stadiums.

PACO: Ooo. I wanna hear all about it.

DIANA: Never. I made it all up. Never happened.

PACO: You weren't a hooker?

DIANA: Don't sound so disappointed. No way, José. Come on. Give me a break. Look at this face. Is this the face of a hooker?

PACO: I never make assumptions.

DIANA: How could you possibly think that of me? Jesus. I thought we were pals. Fuck you, Paco. So, anyway. I moved out to Seattle five years ago or so. And then out here to the beach last summer. I took this job, and there you are.

(Pause)

PACO: I wish I knew when you were kidding.

DIANA: You'll never know.

(Pause)

PACO: Today's not so different, you know.

DIANA: It's not?

PACO: He's kicked before. Once. Came to see me in New York. I was looking forward to it. The return of the gray ghost. Stopped to see his family in Ohio, and showed up hooked again, and out of shit. Shit out of luck. Sat down in my living room and said, first thing, "Paul, I got a problem." Asked my wife to ask her father, who's a doctor, to write a prescription. Which he wasn't too happy about doing. I was in shock. My wife ran all over New York trying to fill that fucking prescription. She got a lot of funny looks, but nobody'd fill it. My father-in-law wrote it so nobody would fill it.

DIANA: Smart.

PACO: Yeah. I gave Ajay some stale Percodans, and took him to see a play.

DIANA: A play?

PACO: I already had the tickets. *Miss Firecracker Contest.* Don't think he cared for it much. Bought him a bottle of Scotch, put him on a plane, sent him packing. Case study, that trip. Anyway, I don't think today's expedition to the Pain Clinic is a done deal.

DIANA: How long were you married?

PACO: Seven years.

DIANA: Sorry.

PACO: Me too. You?

DIANA: Once. One of my clients.

PACO: Stop. You're kidding.

DIANA: You'll never know.

PACO: Damn.

(MAGGIE *comes out of the house onto the porch.*)

PACO: Jesus. Maggie. Have you been in there all this time?

MAGGIE: I heard voices. When did you get in, Paul?

PACO: This morning. Before they left. I saw them off.

MAGGIE: That was thoughtful. I can't come over here anymore while your father's here. He's trying to kill me.

PACO: Maggie.

MAGGIE: He is. He is. He wants to take the money from the lawsuit, and run away to Hawaii with it.

PACO: You've been talking to Aunt Pig again.

MAGGIE: Don't call your Aunt Pig Aunt Pig. Her name's Phyllis. If you can't say something nice

PACO: Ajay is not trying to kill you.

MAGGIE: You don't know. (*Pause*) You're never here. How could you possibly know?

PACO: So, he's running off to Hawaii. With a younger woman.

MAGGIE: Yes, as a matter of fact.

PACO: Please. Ajay doesn't know any younger women. He's been in a drug-soaked stupor for the last twenty years. He knows fewer people than the trip-wire vets hiding out there in the rain forest. Where's he gonna meet a younger woman? At the drug store? The only person he knows any more is his pharmacist.

MAGGIE: He's more devious than you think.

PACO: What do you care anyway? And who could blame him? Why should he live with you the rest of his life?

MAGGIE: Or vice versa.

PACO: Exactly.

MAGGIE: You think it's all my fault?

PACO: No.

MAGGIE: You think I'm responsible for his predicament?

PACO: No.

MAGGIE: After all I've done to keep this family together?

PACO: Oh, please.

MAGGIE: Absconding with my money—

PACO: Your money—

MAGGIE: Mine, by rights, half mine, for putting up with all this for all these years—

PACO: Doing what? Doing what? Nobody asked you, you know. You didn't have to, nobody forced you—

MAGGIE: Taking my money, what's rightfully mine, and deserting me—

PACO: You're getting a divorce—

MAGGIE: Hawaii with some slut—

(PACO *stops short.*)

PACO: I remember distinctly the first time I ever heard that word.

MAGGIE: What word? Hawaii?

PACO: Slut. It was the day after you had the hair-pulling fistfight with Aunt Bug, and you were sitting in the kitchen with Mrs. Harrison, and you called Aunt Bug a slut.

MAGGIE: I did not.

PACO: And Mrs. Harrison thought that was very funny. And I thought it was one of the most fascinating, mysterious, beautiful words I've ever heard. Slut.

MAGGIE: She ran up the phone bill.

PACO: I still think it's a fabulous word. Slut. Took me years to find out what it meant. I knew I couldn't ask you.

MAGGIE: That's not true. I would have told you.

PACO: You didn't have to stick around, you know. You could have gone out and made a new life for yourself.

MAGGIE: How? (*Pause*) You've always been very unforgiving of me, Paul. (*Pause*) Paul, what could I do? I have no training, no skills. All I had was this family.

PACO: Good job you've done of that.

MAGGIE: I did my best. I've done my best.

PACO: Ajay's not going anywhere. He doesn't know any sluts. Young, or otherwise. You ought to have your head examined for listening to Aunt Pig. She's crazier than you. (*To* DIANA) This is what comes of a Catholic boarding school education.

MAGGIE: My education was excellent. And your Aunt Pig's name is Phyllis.

PACO: Agoraphobia. That's what they call what you've got. You ought to get some help.

MAGGIE: Help. The only help I need is a little help around here. There's nothing wrong with me that a little cooperation wouldn't cure.

PACO: You don't live here anymore.

MAGGIE: A little help. Your father's the one who needs help. And your sister, well, she's a case. Two peas in a pod. Thank God for Bubba.

PACO: Bubba's a mess.

MAGGIE: Bubba is a good boy. He has a good job, he helps support Lulu, he's a good egg.

PACO: Right. Look, I'll be back in a sec. I'm just gonna run this stuff down to the trash.

MAGGIE: What is it?

PACO: Nothing. Trash. That's all. *(He exits.)*

MAGGIE: Ajay's dope, that's what it is. Isn't it, Lulu?

DIANA: Diana.

MAGGIE: Diana. Did I call you Lulu? Sorry. I'm upset. First, with Ajay trying to kill me, and then going off to the Pain Clinic, and the divorce and the lawsuit.

DIANA: Change is good. All very positive change.

MAGGIE: I suppose so. I suppose so. We do tend to entropy around this house. To stasis. This latest business about Hawaii. Very upsetting. I don't want to do it. Well, I have no choice. My lawyer says I have no choice. She should know. She's very good. It's going to be very unpleasant.

DIANA: What's that?

MAGGIE: Paul's going to be furious.

DIANA: About what, Maggie?

MAGGIE: Can I trust you? How do I know I can trust you? You seem to be thick as thieves with Paul. He's always been that way. Relies on his charm. Skates through life on his charm.

DIANA: I don't betray confidences. But if you feel that you can't trust me—

MAGGIE: I don't know.

DIANA: Fine. I just thought you were wanting to talk about something. You brought it up. I'd rather not know.

(Pause)

MAGGIE: What do you think of him?

DIANA: Who? Paco?

MAGGIE: Paul.

DIANA: We just met. We're getting along. We're the same age. He's charming.

MAGGIE: Paco. He doesn't look like a Paco. Nobody around here ever called him Paco. He came back from New York calling himself Paco. His friends call him Paco. I won't.

(MAGGIE *exits into the house. When her steps have receded,* PACO *strolls out of the woods.)*

DIANA: Paco. Were you listening to that?

PACO: Just the Paco part. I just didn't want to talk to her again tonight.

DIANA: You don't look like a Paco.

PACO: *En mi corazon. Habla the español?*

DIANA: No.

PACO: Me either. Come on. Let's throw Ajay's junk in the Pacific. I stashed it in the bush.

(DIANA *comes down off the porch.*)

DIANA: Maybe if you're good, I'll tell you about my career as a lady of pleasure.

PACO: Leisure.

DIANA: Leisure and pleasure.

PACO: What else is there?

(PACO *and* DIANA *exit.* MAGGIE *calls from inside the house.*)

MAGGIE: *(Off)* Paul? Paul? Paul? *(She comes out on the porch.)* Paul? Be sure you check the attic. Have you checked the attic? I think he has another ice box full of dope up there. Paul? *(Pause)* Feels like rain. I'm sure. *(Pause)* You think I'm talking just to hear myself talk? *(Pause)* There are clicking sounds on the phone. Your father has tapped the line. You think he's not devious. But he is. *(Pause)* He's not well. I feel sorry for him. *(Pause)* When you kids were little.

(MAGGIE's *words trail off. She stands for a moment, in reverie, then walks down the porch and exits off. Slow fade)*

Scene 3

(Moonlight. More stuff on the porch: a power mower, overstuffed chairs, etc.)

(PACO and DIANA are in the hammock. Making love. They climax. Subsiding sounds)

(A long moment. LULU enters. Starts to come up on the porch. Hears PACO and DIANA. Stops. Peers through the moonlight at the hammock. Sighs. Turns and exits toward the beach.)

(Subsiding sounds subside.)

(Silence)

DIANA: First time for me, you know.

PACO: First time what?

DIANA: In a hammock.

PACO: Oh. Gee. Maybe it was the hammock.

DIANA: Maybe it was, schmuck.

PACO: First time for me, too.

DIANA: In a hammock?

PACO: At the folks. Is that true? I'm not sure. Hard to believe. Maybe not. It's not exactly an erotic atmosphere.

DIANA: Where else? Lovemaking. Unusual places.

PACO: You mean like in front of the Christmas tree at Rockefeller Center?

DIANA: Public places. Kinky spots.

PACO: Let's see. Um. Back seat at the drive-in.

DIANA: That's classic, not kinky.

PACO: That's me to a T. Classic, not kinky. Uh, once in the park at night.

DIANA: Paco.

PACO: No, wait. This is good. Standing up. Against a sequoia.

DIANA: Get serious.

PACO: Once in the middle of The Gifford Pinchot National Forest in broad daylight.

DIANA: God, are you boring.

PACO: Not everyone can be an ex-courtesan.

DIANA: Fuck off.

PACO: Come on, where. I shudder to think.

DIANA: Mmmmm. Once in church. Not during services.

PACO: Whew.

DIANA: A couple of times in a restaurant.

PACO: Oh, my God.

DIANA: You'd be amazed. A long skirt and a dark booth. Yum. Once on the dance floor of a disco.

PACO: Vertical or horizontal?

DIANA: Paco, honestly. Standing up, of course. We were trying to be discreet.

PACO: Oh, I see. Anyone notice?

DIANA: I hope so. Otherwise, what's the point? But we did it so they could pretend not to.

PACO: Worked out well for everyone.

DIANA: It was wonderful.

PACO: Sounds wonderful. Where else?

DIANA: Once on a beach. With two Frenchmen. It was a deserted beach. Once in the Amtrak Vistadome car between Portland and Seattle.

PACO: Somewhere around Chehalis—

DIANA: Somewhere around Chehalis. Once in the ladies' room of the River Café.

PACO: In Brooklyn? Ooo. Interesting. The ladies room. With a man.

DIANA: No.

(*Pause*)

PACO: Oh.

DIANA: It was the times, I guess.

PACO: I understand. The Sixties.

DIANA: Sort of. *(Beat)* Last year.

PACO: Oh. *(Beat)* Still see her?

DIANA: Sometimes. She's married.

(Pause)

PACO: Maybe we should have this conversation later.

DIANA: Okay.

(Pause)

PACO: You know one time Maggie sicced the F B I on her Dad. On Grandpa. It was great. She goes down to New Mexico to visit. Grandpa's seventy-two and working in a car wash. Maggie gets this notion that Grandpa's using the car wash to smuggle cocaine from Mexico in empty beer cans with this friend of his, Mister Peach, who's ninety, if he's a day. We all knew Mister Peach. Grandpa showed up here one day out of the blue with Mister Peach in tow. Driving Mister Peach's vintage apricot Cadillac convertible all the way from Albuquerque. Gimme a shot of Jameson's and a cuppa coffee and I can drive all night, Grandpa'd always say. So that's how we first met Mr. Peach, and he was kinda like a big soft pink pale naked bird, but not that much like a cocaine king. Anyway, Maggie goes down to visit, and comes back convinced she's onto something. Don't ask me why. So she calls the F B I. She goes up to Seattle, and the F B I takes her and my Uncle Fight to lunch. She tells her whole story to this poor guy whose entire job it is to listen to cranks about aliens and U F O abductions and neighbors who are secret North Korean spies, and crackpots like Maggie who are turning in their aging parents as dangerous drug smugglers. And my Uncle Fight tells me later that all the way through lunch he and the F BI guy are rolling their eyes at each other. So you see, there's some precedent for this stuff about Ajay's assassination plot. She's certifiable. Somebody should throw a net over her.

DIANA: That's a funny story. Sad, but funny.

(Pause)

PACO: Some things still surprise me.

DIANA: Like what?

PACO: Bi-sexuality. Its actual, as opposed to mythological, presence in the world.

DIANA: It's not very surprising. It's the opposite.

(Pause)

PACO: Maybe we should have this conversation later.

DIANA: Whenever you want.

PACO: Maybe now's okay.

DIANA: Okay.

PACO: Tell me more. Tell me everything. *(He starts kissing her hair and neck.)*

DIANA: Oh, it turns you on, does it?

PACO: Mmmm. Yes.

DIANA: Mmmm. If you think I'm going to pander to your cheap male fantasies—

PACO: You're not—?

DIANA: You're going to have to be very persuasive.

PACO: I'll do anything—

DIANA: That sounds fair—

PACO: Tell me everything—

DIANA: Mmmm, well—

PACO: In excruciating detail—

DIANA: Okay. But we have to play prove it.

PACO: Prove it—

DIANA: Prove it. Once could be a fluke.

PACO: If we have to—

DIANA: We have to—

PACO: Okay. So. Tell.

DIANA: Okay. We're sitting at a table, in this restaurant—

PACO: The River Café?

DIANA: The River Café—

PACO: Good, cause I know The River Café, I can visualize it. I mean, not the ladies' room, but I know what the men's room looks like—

DIANA: Paco, shut up. You wanna hear this?

PACO: I don't know. It's too exciting. Oh, my, yes, I do. Yes. Yes. Yes. Tell me. Please.

DIANA: Oh, God. Okay. We're at this table, with our dates—

PACO: I can't believe this. With your dates?

DIANA: With our dates. And she's wearing black stockings. And a long black silk shirt. And nothing else.

PACO: How can you tell?

DIANA: An educated guess. I can tell. And she's looking at me. I catch her looking at my—wait.

PACO: What? What are you doing?

(DIANA shifts position, turning her back to PACO.)

PACO: What?

DIANA: While I tell you this. Do my back.

PACO: Okay. (Beat) Do what?

DIANA: Lick. My back.

PACO: Oh. Great. (Beat) Where do I start?

DIANA: At the top. At the nape.

(PACO *does.*)

DIANA: Work your way down. Slowly. Little concentric circles. Be methodical. Be inevitable. Be relentless. Be very—very—thorough. Ooo. Good. That's right. Where was I?

PACO: She's looking at you. At your.

DIANA: Oh, yeah. Not so fast. Take your time. And she's looking at me. Across the table. At my—

(*Pause*)

PACO: At your—?

DIANA: Breasts.

PACO: Ah.

DIANA: And I flush. I feel hot. I can't believe it. At first, I think I'm imagining. And I keep talking to my date. And I catch her. And then I catch her again. And now she knows I know. And she looks at me. Now you know. So? And then she very deliberately looks at my breasts again. And she looks me in the eyes again. And waits. And then I look. At her. At her breasts.

PACO: How do they look?

DIANA: Breath-taking.

PACO: Oh. Oh, my. Maybe we better—

DIANA: Don't stop now.

PACO: Yikes. (*He does her back some more.*)

DIANA: And I look at her breasts for a long time. For what feels to me like a very long time. And then I look up. And she's watching me—watch—her. And she says. Diana. Come with me.

PACO: Grrrrr.

DIANA: And I say yes. I will. But I can't really hear my voice. It sounds like it's coming from another room. And I stand up. And my legs are. And I'm really. Very. Very. Very—

PACO: Yes—?

DIANA: Very much so. And my body feels like it's about to burst into flame. Into blossom. My body is humming. And I start to smile. And I try not to. And I can't stop. And we walk across the room very slowly. And I feel everyone's watching us. And they know. And I watch her. Walking in front of me. Her hips. Moving. And I know her heart is racing, too. And I feel completely happy. Because I know exactly what we're going to do.

(Pause)

PACO: Kiss me.

DIANA: Oh, yes.

(DIANA turns over her shoulders and they kiss and smoulder.)

(LULU enters. Sees and hears them. Stops, sighs.)

LULU: Oh, shit.

(DIANA and PACO disengage.)

PACO: Lulu

LULU: Sorry. I heard voices. Thought it was safe to come back.

PACO: 'S okay. We were just—

DIANA: Just cooling down.

PACO: Yeah

LULU: Really. *(She comes up on the porch.)*

PACO: You were here earlier?

LULU: I took a walk on the beach. Thought you'd be done by now. I'm impressed.

PACO: You coulda just barged on by and gone in the house.

LULU: Yeah, I coulda. Hi, Di. How's tricks?

DIANA: Okay, Lulu. How was your trip?

LULU: How is it in the hammock? Does it work?

DIANA: I highly recommend it.

LULU: I'll have to try it. Some moonlit night.

DIANA: How's Ajay? Is he okay?

LULU: How 'bout the motion? I always thought the motion might be kinda funky. Remember waterbeds? I could never take fucking on waterbeds seriously. Always cracked me up. I'd start laughing, and lose my place—

DIANA: Ah, Lulu. Why don't you like me?

LULU: Who, me? I like you.

DIANA: No, you don't.

(Pause)

LULU: I like you. But you make me nervous.

DIANA: I'm sorry. Excuse me. Would you hand me my clothes?

LULU: Certainly.

(LULU *finds* DIANA*'s things and hands them to her.*)

DIANA: Thanks. *(She gets out of the hammock and exits inside.)*

LULU: Va va voom. Nice bod. For an older woman.

PACO: You're in a good mood.

LULU: Six hours on the road, Paco. I'm beat.

PACO: Why didn't you stay in Seattle?

LULU: Subletting my place.

PACO: So how's Ajay? Really.

LULU: Ajay's okay. I left him there in his regular get-up. Peejays and bathrobe. He looked right at home. They let him keep his pipe.

PACO: Hope he doesn't burn the place down. He looked strange this morning.

LULU: You'd look strange too if you were going off to the Pain Clinic.

PACO: He was dressed. I hadn't seen Ajay dressed in years. Since I don't remember when.

LULU: Well, it looked like a pretty nice place. In spite of the name. Kinda foreboding. The Pain Clinic.

PACO: Good.

LULU: It's right on the edge of campus, at the hospital.

PACO: Where Grandma died.

LULU: Really?

PACO: Really.

LULU: I didn't know that.

PACO: It's true.

LULU: What do you know.

PACO: I thought you knew everything there was to know about the family. And then some.

LULU: What does that mean?

PACO: It means you remember shit I have no recollection of whatsoever, and no way to corroborate. I never know if you're making it up or what.

LULU: Paco, I remember it.

PACO: How do I know that?

LULU: I don't lie.

PACO: How do you know that?

LULU: Paco, please. None of your fancy-ass philosophy at this hour. I'm dead on my feet.

PACO: Okay. Okay. You always tell the truth, and you always remember everything exactly the way it was, and you never embroider.

LULU: I don't fucking embroider. Jesus.

PACO: You know what I don't know?

LULU: Lots.

PACO: I don't know where Jimmy's buried.

LULU: Next to Grandma.

PACO: I know that. But where? It hit me the other day. Right in the middle of *Attack of the Fifty-Foot Woman.* What if you all died or disappeared, how would I find out?

LULU: What do you care, you'd never go anyway.

PACO: No.

LULU: Have you ever been?

PACO: I don't know where it is.

LULU: I'll draw you a map.

PACO: Okay. *(Beat)* Poor Ajay. Can you imagine? Dealing with this shit at sixty.

LULU: He's not sixty.

PACO: So then what? Methadone forever?

LULU: Doctor T says a lot of people kick, eventually.

PACO: And what's supposed to keep him off the hard stuff?

LULU: Therapy. Plus the fact that Clawhammer won't write him a prescription anymore. Since he's suing him. And because of the lawsuit, no doctor in western Washington will so much as write him a Tylenol.

PACO: Another reason for this sudden reformation. How simple of me. How stupid. He's run dry. No more shit.

LULU: Oh, Paco. Who cares? Get off your high horse. He's got a big stash in the house. He's a long way from running dry. He really does want to change.

PACO: I hope so.

LULU: He does.

PACO: Good. Because we threw his shit in the Pacific today.

LULU: No shit?

PACO: No shit.

LULU: Get the refrigerator in the attic?

PACO: Yup.

LULU: Fantastic. I thought somebody should do that.

PACO: Why didn't you?

LULU: I was going to. I was. *(Beat)* Maybe. Or ask Bubba to. *(She stretches and yawns.)* God, I'm tired. I feel like I been rode hard and put away wet.

PACO: Jesus, Lulu. This country living does wonders for your turn of phrase.

LULU: It's colorful, Paco.

PACO: It's scary. All these green-necks and mossbacks and trip-wire vets you hang out with. What do you do for fun around here?

LULU: Drink. Look at the rain. Drive down to the Driftwood. Bitch about the rain. Drink some more. Drive home drunk in the rain. Look at the ocean. Have a nightcap.

PACO: Liquid.

LULU: Soggy. You shoulda seen the size of the slugs this season. You could saddle 'em. We were gonna have a round-up. Brand 'em and drive 'em down the trail to market.

(Pause)

PACO: So. Lulu, sweet Lou, whatcha gonna do?

LULU: Well, Paco. I dunno. There's nothing I want to do. *(Pause)* I am thinking about taking this course in cosmetology.

PACO: That sounds great. Mister Lulu.

LULU: I know. And there's this other thing. Angelic intervention.

PACO: Angelic intervention.

LULU: It's a number of things. Body work. Channel clearing, aura cleansing.

PACO: No.

LULU: Yes. Like when your aura needs cleansing, they analyze it, and then they cleanse it.

PACO: How do they do that?

LULU: Well, I don't know, do I? I haven't taken the course yet. They analyze your aura with some kind of crystal, or something, and see what colors it's picked up, and then they can tell what negative emotions you're holding, and then they cleanse your aura, and you feel better. And your aura looks better to other people, too.

PACO: And that's important.

LULU: Your aura's looking kinda grubby. Maybe if you'd serve real butter with your popcorn down at the Sonoma Roxy.

PACO: I do serve real butter. I don't serve espresso. No espresso, no Haagen-Daz. Strictly real butter and Raisinettes.

(DIANA *comes out in a robe, hair in a towel.*)

DIANA: God, it's unseasonably mild.

LULU: False spring.

PACO: Lulu's been telling me about angelic intervention. The latest thing.

DIANA: Oh, I've heard of that. Aura cleansing.

LULU: And past life clearing.

PACO: Oh, I get it. If you've been bad in some past life, and it's fucking you up in this one, you can have somebody go in and settle your debts. Pay your tab.

LULU: Yeah.

DIANA: Seems like a shortcut to enlightenment.

PACO: Modern times. Buy yourself a do-it-yourself Bohdisattva kit.

LULU: Well, why not, if it can be done.

PACO: Lulu, do you believe in this stuff?

LULU: (*Unsure*) No. But I want to. This lady offered me this job, as an angelic intervention trainee. If I could only get myself to believe this shit, I could take the job.

PACO: You're better off unemployed.

LULU: Easy for you to say.

PACO: Turn around.

LULU: Big thrill.

PACO: Come on.

LULU: Grow up.

PACO: (*To* DIANA) Hand me my clothes, will you?

LULU: God, don't have a cow. B F D.

(LULU *holds her hands over her eyes.* PACO *gets up out of the hammock, gives* DIANA *a quick kiss—)*

LULU: Yuck.

PACO: *(To* DIANA*)* Thanks for pandering.

DIANA: Anytime.

(PACO *picks up his clothes, and exits into the house.)*

DIANA: You gonna take this aura job?

LULU: Probably not. I was telling Paco I might take this course in cosmetology. Move to Hawaii with a skill. If only I could get there without flying.

DIANA: You don't fly?

LULU: Uh uh. No way. Think there's a ferry boat to Honolulu?

DIANA: I doubt it.

LULU: Maybe I'll go crabbing in Alaska. A-lack-sa.

DIANA: How long have you been out of a job?

LULU: Five years.

(DIANA *whistles.)*

LULU: Does that seem like a long time?

DIANA: Yes. Yes, it does.

LULU: Well, I got sick. And then it hasn't been so hot around here, it's a depressed area, a lot of layoffs, the lumber industry's down, and that affects everybody. I was working at an insurance company in Seattle, running the xerox machines, and they liked me, it had good bennies, nice folks, paid okay. But I got sick, missed a lot, and they let me go.

DIANA: What kind of sick?

LULU: You know. Female troubles. Polyps.

DIANA: Benign?

LULU: Yeah. But real unpleasant. They gave me
hormones to get my period going and that made me
feel pretty erratic, and one thing after another, and
a D & C, and finally, couple of months ago, I had a
complete redo, and the doctor told me to forget about
having kids. You know?

DIANA: She sure?

LULU: She's pretty good. I guess it's all sort of a mess
down there. I told Maggie, and you know what she
said? First thing? She said, don't let this be an excuse to
get carried away. (*She laughs.*)

(*Pause*)

DIANA: That's awful.

LULU: I thought it was funny. You wanna get plowed?

DIANA: Oh—

LULU: I got a bottle. Cuervo Gold. Lousy state liquor
control board, can only get the most boring fucking
brands, and they charge you an arm and a leg. I have
a friend, smuggles the most amazing stuff in from
California— (*She's gotten a bottle of tequila from her bag—
) Trailer truckloads of tequila. Herradura Anejo. (—and
offers it to* DIANA.)

DIANA: Maybe a taste. (*She opens it, takes a swig.*)

LULU: Good girl.

(DIANA *hands the bottle back to* LULU.)

LULU: We do this stuff with mushrooms during the
summer. Outrageous. The psylocibin comes out in the
cow pies and elk shit. We go up into the Park around
the Summer Solstice and party for days. (*She takes a
swig.*) Tequila consciousness.

(LULU *gives it back to* DIANA)

DIANA: Thanks. (*She drinks.*)

DIANA: Ooo. Nice. Lime and salt would be nicer.

LULU: Sorry. I hope Ajay's okay.

DIANA: He'll be okay.

LULU: Give me a hit.

(DIANA *hands her the bottle. She takes a long swig.*)

LULU: I'm gonna get wrecked. Wanna get wrecked?

DIANA: No thanks. But I'll watch for a while.

LULU: Fair enough. Wanna smoke?

DIANA: No.

(LULU *rolls a joint.* DIANA *watches her in silence.* LULU *lights up, takes a toke, chases it with a swig of tequila. Exhales. Hands it to* DIANA. DIANA *takes the bottle, swigs.* LULU *holds up the joint.*)

LULU: Sure?

DIANA: Sure.

LULU: I'm gonna get wrecked. *(Pause)* I don't know why you make me nervous.

(*Pause. The fog is beginning to swirl along the base of the porch.*)

LULU: Fog's coming in.

(*Silence.* DIANA *takes another drink, gives the bottle back to* LULU. *She drinks.*)

(*Slow fade*)

END OF ACT ONE

ACT TWO

Scene 4

(The next morning, early. Very foggy. A few more items on the porch.)

(AJAY comes out of the house and down onto the sand. He's still got his traveling clothes on, which have been slept in. He looks gray and tired. He paces a bit.)

(LULU comes out of the house. Pulling on a light jacket, still sleepy and somewhat hungover.)

AJAY: Gonna rain.

LULU: Geez, Pop. Anybody could say that everyday here and be right ninety-five percent of the time.

AJAY: In a hour.

LULU: Okay. *(Pause)* Are you alright?

AJAY: I've got a problem.

(Pause)

LULU: Paco dumped it.

AJAY: Where?

LULU: In the Pacific.

AJAY: I wish he hadn't.

LULU: It's the best thing. *(Beat)* I would have if he hadn't.

AJAY: Are you sure he got it all?

LULU: I think so, Pop.

AJAY: Lulu. Drive me into town, will you?

LULU: Pop. Foreman's isn't open this hour.

AJAY: He's got an emergency number.

LULU: You can't. Mister Foreman'll be furious. 'Member the last time? It makes him crazy. The state's been auditing his books.

AJAY: It's legal.

LULU: Pop, that's not the point.

AJAY: That is the point, for Christ sake. *(Pause)* Paco find the refrigerator?

LULU: Yeah. I think we got it all.

AJAY: Sonuvabitch. I'm gonna be sick. I'm gonna be so sick.

LULU: What can I get you?

AJAY: A little bourbon?

LULU: Tequila.

AJAY: Okay.

(LULU *goes into the house.* AJAY *swallows hard and wipes the sweat off his face with his sleeve. She returns.)*

LULU: Here you go. Take a big swig.

(LULU *hands* AJAY *the bottle. He carefully takes a small sip. Coughs and grimaces. Takes another)*

AJAY: Jesus. How can people drink?

(LULU *laughs. Looks at* AJAY. *Laughs again. Keeps laughing. He eventually smiles a little. She laughs 'til tears come. Wipes her eyes, subsides.)*

LULU: Jeez, Pop, you are a card. You really are.

AJAY: I haven't had tequila since 1948. Your mother and I drove to New Mexico to get married. We were

married by her Uncle Tom. Father Finn. That was
his professional name. Lived way out in the desert
between Albuquerque and Santa Fe. Chama. Well,
not really desert. Don't know what you'd call it. High
chaparral, or something. He ministered to the Indians.
Indians and Spanish. He was a Dominican.

LULU: His name was Father Finnian. And he was a
Franciscan. Feel better?

AJAY: Some. Not much.

LULU: Think you'd better go back.

AJAY: I was feeling pretty bad. Downright awful.

LULU: You'll get used to it.

AJAY: That's what I'm afraid of.

(Pause)

LULU: Mister Foreman knows you're supposed to be at
the Pain Clinic. He's not going to fill your prescription.

AJAY: It's legal. He can't refuse.

LULU: You oughta go back. It'd be the best thing.

AJAY: Yes. Yes, it would.

(Pause)

LULU: I'm too beat to drive back up there again.

AJAY: I could take the bus.

LULU: I called Bubba. He's coming straight from work.

AJAY: He'll be beat.

LULU: Tomorrow's his day off. He stays up `til noon
anyway, and he can spend the night at Aunt Pig's, and
drive back here tomorrow.

AJAY: I don't know.

LULU: Or maybe Paco could drive you.

AJAY: Don't wake Paco. *(Beat)* Where's Diana?

LULU: She's in Paco's room. They're an item.

AJAY: That was fast.

LULU: No kidding.

AJAY: That's nice. *(Pause)* When's he coming?

LULU: Soon. Why'n't you go clean up?

AJAY: Yeah. Okay. Thanks, Lulu.

(It starts to rain, lightly.)

LULU: Hey, Pop. You were right. A little off.

AJAY: I told you. I feel it in my war wounds.

LULU: You weren't wounded in the war.

(AJAY and LULU laugh.)

(AJAY ascends the porch, stops and turns.)

AJAY: Don't tell your mother. More ammo for her.

LULU: Okay, Pop.

AJAY: You know, they took a deposition from her last week, and my lawyers decided not to call her to testify against Clawhammer. They decided she'd be< a hostile witness.

LULU: She's pretty hostile. She's got a lawyer of her own.

AJAY: That's for the divorce.

LULU: When's that supposed to happen?

AJAY: Soon as there's a settlement with Clawhammer.

LULU: Watch out.

AJAY: We've agreed on a formula. We put the principle, whatever the settlement is, in the bank, and split the interest and everything else fifty-fifty. And I buy out her share of this place.

LULU: That seems fair.

AJAY: I think so.

LULU: Won't seem fair to Maggie.

(AJAY *shrugs, and exits into the house.*)

(LULU *smokes a cigarette.*)

(BUBBA *enters. Thirtyish. Wearing a security guard uniform.*)

LULU: You're early.

BUBBA: I told them it was a medical emergency.

LULU: Good.

BUBBA: Where is he?

LULU: Inside. Washing up. He'll be out in a sec.

BUBBA: What happened?

LULU: I think he was lonely.

BUBBA: How'd he get back?

LULU: Caught the dog. The red-eye. Crashed in the Aberdeen bus station for a few hours, `til it got light, then got a cab out here.

BUBBA: How is he? Is he okay?

LULU: Rocky. Kinda rocky.

BUBBA: Why doesn't he take something to tide him over?

LULU: Paco threw it out.

BUBBA: All of it?

LULU: Everything he could find. All of it, I think.

BUBBA: Paco's here, huh?

LULU: Yeah.

BUBBA: How long's he staying?

LULU: I dunno. You know Paco. (*Pause*) How's work?

BUBBA: I might get promoted to sergeant.

LULU: Congratulations. I'm happy for you. Can I borrow some money?

BUBBA: Lulu.

(AJAY *comes out.*)

BUBBA: Hi, Pop.

AJAY: Hi, Bubba.

BUBBA: Ready to roll?

AJAY: Yeah.

BUBBA: Okay.

AJAY: Got enough gas?

BUBBA: Pop.

AJAY: See ya in a month, Lulu.

LULU: See you, Pop. It'll be okay. Hang in there.

BUBBA: `Bye, Lu. Say hi to Paco for me. I haven't seen him since I don't know when.

LULU: He'll be here when you get back.

BUBBA: I wouldn't bet on it. Let's go, Pop.

AJAY: `Bye, Lulu.

LULU: `Bye, Pop.

(AJAY *and* BUBBA *exit. It's raining harder now.* LULU *lights another cigarette and watches the rain come down.*)

LULU: Fucking rain.

(*Slow fade*)

LULU: *Mi vida loca con agua.*

(*Fade out*)

Scene 5

(The next evening. More stuff on the porch, of course.)

(Rain. Wind.)

(LULU comes out on the porch, wraps herself in the hammock blanket.)

(LULU sits. Lights a cigarette.)

LULU: This is a night to be up in the mountains. Driving. What's best is to stop at the top of a ridge, and watch the weather roll in. The fog. Filling up the valleys. Rising up the mountain sides. Coming off the snow like steam. It's real spooky. A night like this, driving, and all you can see is the fog at the edge of the road. And then the edge disappears. And you know the drop is right out there. But you can't see it anymore. A night like this, you think you could lose your life. Nature. Whoosh. *(Pause)* What I like most are the high mountain meadows. Grass. Wildflowers. Stands of pine. Wind. Quiet. Something so sweet. So sweet and faded. You think, I could live here. This is perfect. I could just lie down here for the rest of my life. *(Pause)* They're real fragile. Like an old photograph. *(Pause)* Take your breath away. *(Pause)*

(LULU smokes. BUBBA enters.)

BUBBA: Hi.

LULU: Hi.

BUBBA: Whatcha doing?

LULU: Smoking. Want one?

BUBBA: You better give those up. Coffin nails.

LULU: I quit in January. How's Pop?

BUBBA: He's okay. I signed him back in.

LULU: Were they mad?

BUBBA: I think it's happened before.

LULU: I'll bet. Where'd you stay?

BUBBA: Aunt Pig's.

LULU: How is she?

BUBBA: You know.

LULU: What took you so long?

BUBBA: I picked up a hitchhiker, took him to a reservation. Nice guy. Not very well.

LULU: God, you'll probably get T B or something. Mary Lapadura worked for this lawyer in Hoquiam who got T B from one of his Indian clients.

BUBBA: Lulu. A big I doubt it.

LULU: It's true. Ask her. Guy coughed all the time. Came in and coughed all over her reception area. It was pro bono, too. She quit right away. This guy cough?

BUBBA: Yeah. A lot.

LULU: T B.

BUBBA: Paco still here?

LULU: He and Diana took off. Drove down the coast.

BUBBA: Shoot. Too bad. I wanted to see him.

LULU: Remember when Grandma lived up on the Tulalip reservation? And in the summertime the killer whales would come in the bay, and you could get fresh shrimp from the shrimp boats, and we'd collect jellyfish in a bucket, and dry them on the dock.

BUBBA: No. *(Beat)* And they're orcas. Not killer whales. *(Beat)* Where'd they go?

(MAGGIE *enters, walks up on porch.*)

MAGGIE: Where'd who go?

BUBBA: Paco and Diana.

MAGGIE: Is he gone already?

BUBBA: Yeah.

MAGGIE: Just can't wait to leave, can he? Hello, Bubba.

BUBBA: Hi, Ma.

LULU: Sonoma, I guess.

MAGGIE: I've never been to California. How's work?

LULU: He might get promoted.

MAGGIE: Good.

BUBBA: I might get transferred, too.

MAGGIE: Where?

BUBBA: The company has malls all over the Midwest. And Georgia.

MAGGIE: You could visit your cousins in Toledo.

BUBBA: Oh, boy.

MAGGIE: A change would be good for you.

BUBBA: They wanted to transfer me to Anchorage, but I said no way.

LULU: You passed up a chance to go to Alaska? I can't believe it.

BUBBA: It's really expensive.

LULU: So?

BUBBA: You know how much a quart of milk costs in Alaska?

LULU: I don't wanna know. I don't drink milk.

BUBBA: You have to live in a quonset hut.

LULU: You do not. They don't have quonset huts. It's too cold.

MAGGIE: I hope you take the next one they offer, Bubba.

BUBBA: Have to. If I don't, they'll fire me.

LULU: I want to go crabbing in Alacksa.

BUBBA: Alaska.

LULU: I know.

MAGGIE: Change of scene.

BUBBA: They've invested a lot in my future. You can see their point. Management training. My company's on the cutting edge of mall security. Retail merchandise control. Traffic flow. Employee pilferage. It's an expanding field. New wrinkles. New technology. There's a lot to keep abreast of. It's a field with a future. And you meet a lot of interesting people.

LULU: Shoplifters.

BUBBA: Every day is different.

MAGGIE: I've never been to Alaska, either. I've been to Denver. To see your Uncle Tug and the twins. I've been to Albuquerque. (*Pause*) The place I've always wanted to go is Budapest. (*Pause*) Your father used to travel. In his business. When you kids were little. Boondoggles. I always stayed home. (*Pause*) What choice did I have? It wasn't an issue.

(*Pause*)

LULU: Remember when Ajay brought home those pecan candy things from New Orleans?

BUBBA: Pralines.

MAGGIE: Pure butter and sugar.

LULU: I like 'em.

MAGGIE: No wonder his teeth are shot. (*Pause*) Your father came home from New Orleans. I'll never forget. He'd never been to the South before. Except the year we lived in Lubbock. Before Paul was born. Your father was in graduate school, and I acquired a terrible Texas accent. It was awful. Protective coloration. Everything was covered with a fine red dust. You could run your finger along any surface. And there wasn't a tree in West Texas. Not a tree to be seen. Took me a year to get rid of that twang. *(Beat)* Your father went to New Orleans. This was 1959 or so. Before everything. And he went to a hambuger stand for dinner. Only your father would go to a hamburger stand in New Orleans. Your father would go to a hamburger stand in Paris. And he's standing in line behind a black man. And they were very rude to him. They served him, but they were rude. And he didn't say anything, the black man. He just held his peace. Paid for his hamburger and left. Made quite an impression on your father. Came home all shook up. Said he'd never realized. Said imagine dealing with that sort of thing. Day in and day out. *(Pause)* Only progressive political sentiment I ever heard him utter. We used to have the most terrible fights.

LULU: We remember.

MAGGIE: About Civil Rights. The Civil Rights Movement. About the riots. Politics. Feminism. About the war. Especially about the war. Thank God Paul wasn't drafted. Even if he did squander his student deferment and his scholarship money. Terrible fights. From the beginning. I was always a Democrat. Well. It was a mixed marriage. My mother warned me about mixed marriages.

(Pause)

LULU: Tell me something, Maggie—

MAGGIE: I wish you wouldn't call me Maggie. I'm your mother.

LULU: Why'd you marry him? I've always wondered.

MAGGIE: I don't know. I never loved him. *(Pause)* I had to get away. *(Pause)* Prague. In April. *(Pause)* Day in and day out.

(They sit in silence.)

(Slow fade)

Scene 6

(Three and half weeks later)

(A late gray afternoon)

(DIANA comes out of the house, onto the porch. Looks.)

(PACO comes from off, toward the beach.)

PACO: Any sign of 'em?

DIANA: Not yet.

PACO: They're late.

DIANA: Paco.

PACO: Right. *(He joins DIANA on the porch.)*

DIANA: They'll be here.

PACO: Yeah.

(Pause)

PACO: There we were. A snowy January morning. Which kept the whole thing feeling like a dream to me. It never snows here. Hardly ever. Almost never. But it had snowed, the night before, and Maggie's crying, been crying non-stop for three days and we're standing around the station wagon watching our breath, numb and dreaming, Lulu, Bubba and me, and Ajay's inside in his usual stupor, trying to pull himself together. And the appointed hour is upon us, and Maggie finally stops crying long enough to say "One of you go in and get your father," and I look at Bubba and Lulu, and they look at me, and we start laughing. It occurs to us all at the same moment. The family joke about Ajay being late to his own funeral. We get hysterical. We laughed and laughed, as they say. And Maggie's getting more and more upset, and then Ajay finally comes out of the house, and he's furious. What are you bastards laughing at? This isn't a funny day. *(Pause)* But it was. It was a very funny day.

DIANA: Beyond embarrassment.

PACO: Beyond embarrassment.

(DIANA kisses PACO.)

PACO: Today's different.

DIANA: Yes, it is.

(DIANA and PACO kiss again. He nods, looks around the porch.)

PACO: Where does this stuff come from? I swear, stuff clones in this house. Listen, we should go up peninsula tomorrow. Up to the Cape. Go geoducking. Know geoducks?

DIANA: Geoducks? No.

PACO: It's a Chinook word. Means ugliest creature on earth. Giant burrowing clam. Looks like a big, thick slab of something nasty. Yuck. Better yet, we could go to Pysht.

DIANA: You really know how to show a girl a good time.

PACO: Washington has the best place names. Easy. Pysht. Sequim. Puyallup. Queets. Quinalt. Nisqually. Snohomish. Skykomish. Sammamish. Duwamish. Squamish. Ohanepecosh. Okanogan. Snoqualmie. Clallam. Moclips. Issaquah. Enumclaw. Walla Walla. Klickitat. Nooksack. Skookumchuck. Humptulips.

DIANA: You made that one up.

PACO: No. I didn't.

DIANA: There are a lot of places I'd like to go.

PACO: Say the word and I'll take you to Sequim.

DIANA: Nor Humptulips neither. *(Pause)* Every so often I get the urge to leave my life behind. Burn my credit cards. Cut my hair. Change my name. Light out for the territory. Just vaporize the past. Turn it into petroglyphs. *(Pause)* On the lam. Get a goddamned big car and a secret tattoo and drive to Mexico using an alias. '55 Ford Fairlane goin' for broke. Dark glasses and Coca-colas. Salty sweat and sticky shirts and big radio. And the heat shimmer on the desert highway rising in the distance like the dream of a better life. *(Beat)* Down through Sonora. Guaymas. Mazatlan. Run out of road in San Blas. Where pirates with parrots perched on their shoulders sit in cafes drinking shots of mezcal. And flamingos meander. And there's a lagoon near San Blas where the waves break in perfect sequence down the sand. And the pelicans catch the thermals, and ride motionless between teal blue water and jade green jungle mountain. Rising into the endless Mexican sky. *(Beat)* And there's an old man, rocking along on a burro cart. Dozing under his hat. And we stop and ask him. What is this place called? And he smiles and says, "Cielitos". Paradise. Little Paradise. Little Skies. *(Pause)* My house burst into flame. My life. I lost everything. Books, papers, letters, photographs, clothes. All my numbers. Everything. It was a little coach house behind the main house. And I came home at two in the morning, and there were firetrucks and firemen with axes everywhere. Revolving red lights. Streams of ice. It was the middle of winter. Big clouds of breath. And I walked up the alley. And my little house was just a mass of sodden, smoking debris. And this fireman said, "This your place, Miss?" And I said, "yes." And he said, "Sorry. We had to chop through your roof." *(Pause)* I spent the night with a friend. The clothes on my back, the shoes on my feet. And in the morning I woke up. And I felt. Dazzled. Stripped. Like I had a new skin. Like I had no skin. Like I'd sloughed off my old life, and stepped out into the sunlight, all wet and shining. Naked and new. *(Beat)* And the next day I left town.

(Pause)

PACO: Which town was that?

DIANA: It isn't there anymore. *(Pause)* There are a lot of places I'd like to go. I'd like to go to Katmandu and stay at the Yak and Yeti. I'd like to go to Truk. I'd like to go to Yap.

PACO: Where they?

DIANA: South Pacific. I'd like to go to The Maldives. The Marquesas. Isla Mujeres. I'd like to go to an island on the other side of the world, with a pink sand beach and a coral reef and sit in an open-air palm-thatched bar and watch the sunset for a year or two and drink rainbow-colored rum drinks and every so often have my way with you.

PACO: Sounds grim.

(DIANA and PACO kiss. LULU enters from off, walks up on porch.)

LULU: When're you guys gonna cool the sex thing? I mean, it's been a month already. Take it from me, middle-aged passion is not a pretty sight.

(DIANA and PACO break kiss. DIANA fixes LULU.)

DIANA: Lulu, why don't you fly?

LULU: Excuse me?

DIANA: I'm wondering why you won't fly.

LULU: Scares me.

DIANA: Have you ever flown?

LULU: No.

DIANA: Then how do you know you're afraid of flying?

LULU: I can imagine.

(Sounds of a car pulling up.)

DIANA: I hear them.

LULU: Do you think he'll want dinner?

DIANA: I don't know.

LULU: I bought him some Snickers bars.

PACO: Oh, God, Lulu—

LULU: Paco, he likes 'em.

PACO: He won't need all that sweet shit now. I hope.

DIANA: Do you think he can even eat Snickers?

LULU: Sure. Those new choppers are excellent.

PACO: New teeth. Thought he looked different.

DIANA: Takes ten years off him.

LULU: At least he stopped dying his hair with shoe polish. That was the worst. Ajay. What a card.

(LULU and PACO laugh.)

(AJAY and BUBBA enter. AJAY looks drawn and gray.)

PACO: Hey, Pop.

DIANA: Hi, Ajay. Welcome home.

LULU: Pop.

AJAY: Paco. Diana. Lulu. What's the big joke?

LULU: I was remembering the cordovan shoe polish you used to put in your hair.

AJAY: My salad days.

LULU: Remember the time you convinced me to put fish fertilizer on my hair? Paco stopped me just before I was about to pour it on my head.

AJAY: You did put something on your hair turned it green once.

LULU: Copper polish.

AJAY: Copper polish.

PACO: Hi, Bubba.

BUBBA: Hi, Paco.

PACO: Long time no see.

BUBBA: Yeah. How are you, Diana?

DIANA: I'm okay, Bubba. How are you?

BUBBA: Good. The drive down was uneventful. It stopped raining once we got to Chehalis.

DIANA: I like Chehalis.

BUBBA: How was Sonoma?

DIANA: Wonderful. I saw Paco's theater. Which was stunningly gorgeous.

BUBBA: Really. Wow. What was playing?

DIANA: *Slither.*

BUBBA: That's a good movie.

DIANA: Well—

(Pause)

PACO: How are you, Ajay?

AJAY: I feel like shit.

PACO: Good.

AJAY: Like a persistent, low-grade flu.

PACO: That's what you expected, right?

AJAY: Expecting is one thing, living it is something else.

PACO: I'm sure it is.

AJAY: Supposed to get better. Eventually. Up to a point.

LULU: Are you hungry, Pop?

AJAY: No.

LULU: I bought you some Snickers.

BUBBA: Oh, Lulu, gross.

LULU: Shut up.

AJAY: I'll take a rain check.

LULU: I could whip you up some s'mores.

AJAY: Maybe later, Lulu. Think I'll take a load off. *(He crawls over some stuff and into the hammock.)*

DIANA: Let me put your stuff inside for you. *(She takes his bag inside.)*

PACO: So, Bubba, how are you?

BUBBA: Pretty good, Paco. Can't complain. My company just made me a sergeant.

PACO: Great.

LULU: He's gonna loan me some money.

BUBBA: Probably. Against my better judgment.

PACO: Lulu tells me you've got a girlfriend.

BUBBA: Well, I was seeing this woman. She had a six-year-old kid. That was sort of interesting. She told me she wanted to stay friends. They all say that. So. Easy come, easy go.

PACO: I'm sorry.

BUBBA: No problem.

LULU: Tell him about the one before that.

BUBBA: Oh, yeah. She had direct communication with Ethel Merman in the spirit world.

PACO: Really.

BUBBA: Yeah. The Merm. The Merm spoke to her. The Merm and Bob Marley.

PACO: Oh, boy.

BUBBA: What about you? How's the movie biz?

PACO: It was still there a week ago. Right now it's *Attack of the Crab Monsters* held over, second smash week.

BUBBA: That's one of my favorites.

PACO: Mine too.

LULU: Mine too. I used to hide my eyes when it was on T V. You and Jimmy used to pretend you had turned into crab monsters and were going to eat me up.

PACO: God, you had a traumatic childhood.

LULU: Tell me about it.

BUBBA: You used to tell me the owls were going to come and pluck out my eyes and carry me off.

PACO: I did? Jesus, that's horrible. Did you believe me?

BUBBA: No. Paco, have you heard about these trip-wire vets?

PACO: Yeah.

BUBBA: They're amazing. They live up in the National Park and live off the land. They don't talk to anybody for months at a time. They shoot elk with bows and arrows. They can't build fires, so they have to eat the meat raw so the rangers don't find them.

PACO: You gonna do that?

BUBBA: I'm not a vet.

LULU: He'd like to be. He'd like to kill poor defenseless deer for breakfast. Bambi for breakfast. God, how'd we ever get such a little fascist for a baby brother?

BUBBA: I'm not a fascist.

PACO: He's not a fascist, Lulu.

LULU: You should see his apartment. Guns, war games, military history books. He's got the complete Time-Life World War II videos. He's a fascist.

AJAY: Who's a fascist?

LULU: Bubba.

AJAY: Bubba's not a fascist. He's a security guard.

LULU: Same difference. If he's not a fascist, he's a control freak. What are you afraid of, Bubba? The dark? Pop, you ready for a Snickers?

AJAY: No thanks.

(LULU *exits into the house.*)

BUBBA: Boy. Sometimes she just goes off.

PACO: Yeah. So. Pop. You wanna talk about it?

AJAY: No. Not now, Paco. Not now.

PACO: Okay.

AJAY: Maybe tomorrow. Okay?

PACO: Okay.

(*Pause*)

AJAY: Quite a collection of misfits, I will say that.

PACO: Yeah?

(*Long pause.* PACO *looks at* BUBBA. *Has he fallen asleep? They make a move to go inside. Then:*)

AJAY: Quite a collection. Dregs of society. Lawyers. Dope dealers. Businessmen. Basketball players. A couple of shrinks. Pack of liars and thieves. Pretty entertaining bunch.

(*Long pause. He's out.* PACO *goes inside.* BUBBA *follows.*)

(*Slow fade*)

Scene 7

(The next morning. Sea birds. Sunlight.)

*(*DIANA *and* PACO *are sitting on the porch.)*

PACO: My theory is. My theory is Ajay was the second gunman. In Dallas. On the grassy knoll.

DIANA: Paco.

PACO: C I A all the way. Makes sense. Timing's right. It was after '63 he started to go to pieces. Couldn't stand the guilt. *(Pause)* I used to deal a little. In college. For book money. I was a lousy poker player, so—

DIANA: What'd you deal?

PACO: This and that. A little acid, a little grass. Assorted hallucinogens. Not speed, `cause everyone got that legally at the infirmary. And not hard stuff. I couldn't. Couldn't stand the symmetry.

DIANA: Did you not do drugs, too? Because of Ajay?

PACO: No, I did them. Not a lot, but every once in a while. One time Ajay gave me and Jimmy a heartfelt lecture on the evils of marijuana. It was hard to take seriously. Considering the source. *(Beat)* I still get the urge. Every once in a while. A yearning for that oceanic feeling.

DIANA: So do I.

PACO: Let's drop acid, babe.

DIANA: Dude. *(Pause)* What do you miss most about being married?

PACO: Seders.

DIANA: Seders?

PACO: Seders. She was Jewish. Is. My ex. *(Beat)* You?

DIANA: Am I Jewish?

PACO: What do you miss most about being married?

DIANA: Dancing `til dawn.

PACO: Oh. That kind of marriage. We could do that.

DIANA: I don't see why not.

PACO: Are you Jewish?

(Pause)

DIANA: I haven't danced `til dawn in years.

PACO: I haven't stayed up all night in years.

DIANA: I haven't dropped acid in years.

PACO: I haven't driven cross-country in years.

DIANA: I haven't hitch-hiked in years.

PACO: I haven't slept with a stranger in years.

DIANA: Paco—

PACO: Except you. And you're not a stranger. I just don't know anything about you.

DIANA: Yes you do. *(Beat)* The world's different. More dangerous.

PACO: The world's always dangerous. We're just getting old. *(Pause)* I don't know what I expected. *(Pause)* I guess I thought he'd walk in here and be his old self. The one I remember. The one I think I remember. Strong and handsome and young. I guess I thought he'd reappear. Pick me up in his arms and spin me through the air. And I'd laugh. And he'd spin me faster and faster. And then he'd let go. And I'd go sailing into the sky. Towards the sun. Waving. Goodbye. Goodbye. And it would be okay. It would all be okay. *(Pause)* I guess I expected the fucking fountain of youth.

DIANA: Paco, it's a start.

PACO: Yeah.

DIANA: He's better.

(MAGGIE *enters, walks up to the porch.*)

MAGGIE: Who's better?

DIANA: Ajay.

MAGGIE: Is he here?

DIANA: Yes.

MAGGIE: I'd like to see him. Diana, would you mind?

DIANA: No. Not at all. (*She exits into the house.*)

MAGGIE: Hello, Paul.

PACO: Hello, Maggie.

MAGGIE: When did you get back?

PACO: A few days ago.

MAGGIE: Why haven't you called? Why haven't you come to see me?

PACO: I'm sorry. I've been helping Diana get the house in order.

MAGGIE: What is all this stuff on the porch? Things fall apart when I'm not around.

PACO: That's funny. The Empress of Entropy. The Queen of Chaos.

(AJAY *comes out of the house, followed by* BUBBA.)

AJAY: Maggie.

MAGGIE: Ajay. You're back from the clinic?

AJAY: Yeah.

MAGGIE: It went alright?

AJAY: Yeah. I guess so.

MAGGIE: Does that mean you're on methadone now?

AJAY: That's right. A maintenance dose.

MAGGIE: For how long?

(AJAY *shrugs.*)

MAGGIE: Forever?

AJAY: I hope not.

MAGGIE: Well, don't set your sights too high. It's awfully hard to kick something like that, like what you had, so many years, completely. You ought to thank your lucky stars for Doctor T.

AJAY: Every day and every night.

(Pause)

MAGGIE: Bubba, how's Shelley?

BUBBA: She's okay. She just wants to be friends.

MAGGIE: Oh, what a shame.

BUBBA: No problem.

MAGGIE: Bubba, would you go park my car for me? I think it's in the flower bed.

BUBBA: You shouldn't drive without a license. It's against the law.

MAGGIE: Be a good egg. Thanks.

(BUBBA exits.)

MAGGIE: Paul. I need to talk to your father.

PACO: Okay. *(He goes into the house.)*

MAGGIE: I'm happy for you, Ajay. I really am.

AJAY: If it works out.

MAGGIE: It might.

AJAY: I hope so.

(Pause)

MAGGIE: My lawyer tells me Clawhammer's offered to settle.

AJAY: I'm afraid so.

MAGGIE: What do you mean?

AJAY: It's not much. A fraction of what I asked.

MAGGIE: A bird in the hand.

AJAY: That's what Wines said.

MAGGIE: Juries are very risky. Unpredictable.

AJAY: Wines said that, too. If I'd known you were a lawyer, I wouldn't have had to hire Wines.

MAGGIE: My lawyer says one twenty-five.

AJAY: After Wines takes his forty percent. You're pretty up to date.

MAGGIE: I know you signed the papers yesterday in Seattle.

(Pause)

AJAY: We have an agreement, Maggie.

MAGGIE: I want my share. I deserve it.

AJAY: Don't be stupid. For once. It's worth more to both of us this way. We talked about this.

MAGGIE: I don't trust you, Ajay. I don't want you disappearing with my share. I know you. I want a little peace of mind in my old age.

AJAY: I'm not going anywhere.

MAGGIE: I can manage my own money.

AJAY: Sure you can.

MAGGIE: I'm not going to be dependent. *(Pause)* I'm filing a lawsuit. I'm suing you, Ajay. I'm asking for the whole settlement.

(Pause)

AJAY: You'll end up with less.

MAGGIE: Haven't I always? *(Pause)* Thirty-five years.

AJAY: Don't pretend you did what you did for me.

MAGGIE: Well, I certainly didn't do it for me.

(Pause)

AJAY: You still blame me for Jimmy.

MAGGIE: They weren't mine, Ajay. He didn't get them from me.

(Pause)

(LULU *comes out on the porch.*)

LULU: Phone's for you, Pop. Mister Wines' office calling from Seattle.

(LULU *hands* AJAY *a Snickers bar.* AJAY *unwraps it, takes a bite. Chews it contemplatively. Looks at* MAGGIE)

AJAY: Goddamn you, Maggie. *(He goes into the house.)*

LULU: I wish you guys would get a divorce already. It's giving me an ulcer.

MAGGIE: Divorce is very hard on adult children.

LULU: Where'd you read that? *Cosmo*?

MAGGIE: I am alone in this family. Alone.

LULU: Mother. What are you talking about?

MAGGIE: I've always been alone. Lulu. Whom do you blame?

LULU: For what?

MAGGIE: For everything.

LULU: God?

MAGGIE: Don't be smart, Miss Lucy. For Jimmy.

(Pause)

LULU: Jimmy. Who else?

(MAGGIE *sighs.*)

MAGGIE: I have such fond memories of when you kids were little.

(Pause)

(PACO *comes out of the house.*)

PACO: Words fail me.

MAGGIE: Paul. I knew you'd be furious.

PACO: Your timing is exquisite. Ambush him as he comes out of rehab. You just can't stand—

MAGGIE: Paul, you don't know my side of the story—

PACO: You just can't stand it, can you? To see him get better.

MAGGIE: He decides he wants to change his life. He wants to get a divorce. What about me? Where's my say in this?

PACO: You want one too. You need one too.

MAGGIE: I need the money, Paul. I deserve it. You have always taken your father's side.

PACO: That's what he used to say about me and you.

MAGGIE: I deserve that money, Paul. You don't know what it was like.

PACO: I know.

MAGGIE: You weren't here. You don't know.

PACO: Okay. I don't know.

MAGGIE: When your Aunt Pig threw that surprise twenty-fifth wedding anniversary party for your father and me, I thought I was going to throw up. The one you didn't bother to come to.

PACO: I didn't know what to buy for a present.

MAGGIE: Something silver. Or pewter.

(*Pause*)

PACO: I am so furious with you. I may never speak to you again.

MAGGIE: I hope that doesn't happen.

PACO: It's going to take something like that to get through to you.

MAGGIE: How are you going to get through to me if you quit speaking to me? *(To* LULU*)* Goodbye.

LULU: Want me to drive you home?

MAGGIE: Bubba can do it. Goodbye, Paul.

PACO: Go away, Maggie.

(Pause)

MAGGIE: When are you leaving?

PACO: Tomorrow.

MAGGIE: Call me.

*(*PACO *shrugs.* MAGGIE *exits off. Pause)*

LULU: I'm going to make s'mores. You want some? I ran out of marshmallow cream, so I'm using Miracle Whip.

*(*PACO *doesn't answer.* LULU *goes in the house. After a moment,* DIANA *comes out.)*

DIANA: Hi.

PACO: Hi. Did you hear?

DIANA: Yes.

PACO: So predictable.

DIANA: I know. Awful. But I think she has a point.

PACO: What point is that?

DIANA: She suffered, too.

PACO: She gave more than she got.

(Pause)

DIANA: Paco, you ought to have more compassion for your mother.

PACO: Where's it written? *(Pause)* Friend of mine has an Irish mother, too. He says the Oedipal theory is true. Boys do want to sleep with their mothers. Except for boys with Irish mothers. They want to sleep with other people's mothers.

DIANA: But seriously.

PACO: I'm going back to Sebastapol tomorrow.

DIANA: Check on the crab monsters?

PACO: Yeah. Wanna come?

DIANA: Maybe. Don't want to leave Ajay in the lurch.

PACO: Ajay'll be okay.

DIANA: Yeah.

PACO: Summer's coming. Summer in Sonoma.

DIANA: Summer in Sonoma. Sounds tempting.

PACO: Prettiest place on earth.

DIANA: Were you in Sonoma that summer? Did you see the running fence? Christo's running fence?

PACO: Oh, yes.

DIANA: I think that's the most beautiful thing I've ever seen. Those two weeks it was up. The running fence at sunset. Running over the hills to the sea.

PACO: I was in Sonoma that summer.

DIANA: And the lunar eclipse?

PACO: I remember.

DIANA: We drove out and looked at the fence. The eclipse turned it menstrual red. The whole world was menstrual red. Washed in moonblood.

PACO: That was the same summer I saw a woman from the Manson family in a Petaluma laundromat, doing her laundry. She had a little X carved in her forehead.

DIANA: Oh, Paco.

PACO: Quite a summer. Ran the gamut.

DIANA: I haven't spent a summer in Sonoma in years. It's very tempting.

PACO: So are you. *(Beat)* Diana. Come with me.

DIANA: Grrrrrrr.

(DIANA and PACO kiss. They kiss passionately. They fall off the porch into the sand, still kissing.)

(They break kiss.)

DIANA: I know this deserted beach.

PACO: I haven't danced 'til dawn on a deserted beach in years.

DIANA: Oh, yes.

(DIANA and PACO kiss again. They get up. They exit toward the beach. AJAY comes out of the house, dressed in his robe and peejays. He has a small velvet box in his hand. He sits on the porch and smokes his pipe. After a moment, BUBBA enters, sits across from AJAY. AJAY hands him the box. BUBBA opens it.)

BUBBA: Wow. *(Looks at AJAY.)* Pop. *(He takes a medal out of box, admires it.)* Bronze star. *(Looks at AJAY.)*

AJAY: I was eighteen, and afraid they were gonna win the war without me. After graduation, I took a bus into Toledo and went to the Navy recruiter and tried to enlist. They turned me down. Flat feet. I went across the street to the Army recruiting office and scrunched my foot up so I had arches. Next thing I knew I was parachuting into the Ardennes in the dead of winter I've never been so cold in my life. During the Battle of the Bulge, my platoon leader got killed. They made me acting sergeant and put me behind a heavy machine gun. It was very confusing. Fog. Snow. You couldn't see anything. I shot at some Germans, but I don't know if I hit anyone. I was evacuated, hospitalized with frostbite and hepatitis. *(Beat)* In the hospital, they gave me the Bronze Star. *(Beat)* Never told me why, exactly. *(Beat)* Never felt right a day in my life since. *(Beat)* I got out, came home, met your mother. *(Pause)* I often wonder. If I'd had the presence of mind. To pass that first physical. What would have happened? If I'd gone in the Navy. I might've shipped out to the Pacific. I might have been killed. I might not have gotten sick. I might have had a whole other life.

(Pause)

(BUBBA looks at AJAY, nods. Holds box out to him. AJAY demurs. Gestures for him to keep the medal. BUBBA nods again, looks at the medal.)

(They sit in silence a moment. LULU comes out of the house with a plate of s'mores.)

LULU: Bubba?

BUBBA: Thanks.

(LULU offers them to AJAY.)

LULU: S'mores, Pop?

(AJAY takes one. LULU sits down on the steps next to BUBBA.)

(They watch the sunset silently.)

(Slow fade)

END OF PLAY